1 Hour From Success

How to Start Your Online Business, Increase Sales, Drive Traffic, and Please Your Customers

By Mike Raft,

Online Business Owner with over $1.8 Million in Sales.

Copyright /Disclaimer

Copyright 2018

This publication is not intended to provide any legal advice; please seek a lawyer for legal advice. I am not a lawyer. To ensure you are protected by local laws in your country you should talk to a licensed attorney or check with the appropriate government agency before using any of the following information in this publication.

This publication can be printed by the purchaser, for use by the purchaser only. Otherwise, no part of this publication may be reproduced or transmitted in any form or by any means, electronic or mechanical, including photocopying, recording or by any information storage and retrieval system, without written permission from the author, except as permitted by U.S. copyright law.

The information provided within this publication is for general informational purposes only. While we try to keep the information up-to-date and correct, there are no representations or warranties, express or implied, about the completeness, accuracy, reliability, suitability or availability with respect to the information, products, services, or related graphics contained in this publication for any purpose. Any use of this information is at your own risk.

The methods described in this publication are the author's personal thoughts. They are not intended to be a definitive set of instructions for this project. You may discover there are other methods and materials to accomplish the same end result.

The information contained within this publication is strictly for educational purposes. If you wish to apply ideas contained in this publication, you are taking full responsibility for your actions.

The author has made every effort to ensure the accuracy of the information within this publication was correct at time of publication. The author does not assume and hereby disclaims any liability to any party for any loss, damage, or disruption caused by errors or omissions, whether such errors or omissions result from accident, negligence, or any other cause.

This publication and the content provided herein are simply for educational purposes and do not take the place of legal advice from your attorney. Every effort has been made to ensure that the content provided is accurate and helpful for our readers at publishing time. However, this is not an exhaustive treatment of the subjects. No liability is assumed for losses or damages due to the information provided. You are responsible for your own choices, actions, and results. You should consult your attorney for your specific questions and needs.

Table of Contents

My Story 6
Introduction 11
   List of things you will learn 13
Chapter 1 15
Recipe for Success 15
   Do you have the ingredients? 15
Business Startup Checklist 17
Income and Expense Checklist 21
Chapter 2 24
Getting Started 24
   Title, tags, and description/SEO optimization 26
SEO Checklist 32
Listing Images 34
   Policies 35
   Branding 38
Chapter 3 39
Growing Your Shop 39
Advertising Checklist 40
   Getting the most from your advertising 42
Chapter 4 46
Problems Arrive 46

    Unhappy customers: Reviews and cases 46

    Copyright claims, DCMA 49

Chapter 5 50

Shipping 50

    Pricing 50

    Packaging 51

Final Checklist 54

Chapter 6 56

Final Words 56

My Story

My story starts in the middle of the "Great Recession." It was 2009, and my family had just moved to Portland, OR from Austin, TX. I needed a job. I had been in the construction and remodeling industry for nearly my entire working life (I was 30 years old), and I'd made good money… until the housing bust hit. My wife had also made good money. She had been a Realtor when real estate was going strong. However, after the economic downturn, even her former boss was working as a cashier at the grocery store. So, I began applying for every job for which I was qualified. I even applied for jobs for which I wasn't qualified...

Several weeks went by, and I started getting nervous about what the future might hold. Finally, after having applied for hundreds of job openings, I landed an interview. The position was for "facilities maintenance" at a high-rise in downtown Portland. I was excited to finally have landed an interview and had high hopes for what might be an excellent opportunity. I went downtown, found the place, went up to the 20th floor and came in to meet the people who would be interviewing me. We sat down and they asked me about my work experience. I talked about myself, bragging about my qualifications as much as I could.

I thought everything was going well, but as the interview neared its end, they told me how slim my odds were for getting the position. They said, "It's amazing the response we've had for this maintenance position. We've had hundreds of resumes come in. We even got a resume from a licensed attorney, and we have an interview with him later today. We've had all kinds of professionals apply for this position. It's going to be hard for us to narrow it down. Well, thanks for coming in; we will call you if we want you to come in for a second interview."

I was starting to realize that I was in a dire situation. The economy was horrible, and everybody and their brother was looking for a job.

A few weeks later, I landed a low-paying maintenance job. We scraped by for the next few years, with barely enough money to pay the bills. I was desperate to find something better to support our family, but I lacked the knowledge and inspiration to break out of my rut. There is a saying: "Success is 10% inspiration and 90% perspiration." However, it was the 10% inspiration that motivated me to put in the 90% perspiration (i.e., hard work) necessary to achieve my goal.

The summer of 2011 marked a significant turning point in my life. I read a book that my wife, Amy, had recommended to me: *Your Money or Your*

Life, by Vicki Robin and Joe Dominguez. I recommend this book to anyone seeking to enhance their perspective on their career and financial situation. For me, this book was a game-changer. As I progressed through it, I began looking at my life differently. The book opened my eyes to the actual value of my time. In some ways, I had been living my life unconsciously. This book was the Holy Grail that set me on a new path. If it hadn't been for this book, I don't think I would have started my online business.

In the meantime, my wife was selling items online, things she found at garage sales and thrift stores. She would find a pair of boots at a garage sale for $5 and resell them on Etsy for $45. She was making a significant profit. I saw the potential, so I started helping her on the weekends and whenever I had time. She was doing most of the work, but after six months or so, we were making over $1,000 month, working only a couple of hours a day. If it weren't for my wife, I wouldn't have seen the potential that awaited us. She was another critical component that set the events in motion for our future online business.

One day, when I was helping my wife add new items to her shop, I browsed through Etsy. I noticed that people were selling stump tables for $100 each. We had access to some reclaimed logs, so

I started my own Etsy shop. I bought a chainsaw and started building stump tables...

Before I knew it, I had listed five stump tables, and sold them all for around $100 each, all while working out of a small one-car garage. I was starting to see how much demand existed for these items. I still had a full-time job, so I had time to work on my business only on the evenings and weekends.

Over the next year or so, I created a GoDaddy website and Facebook page. I moved into a bigger shop and continued to make stump tables and other furniture on the weekends. When I was sure I could make a living, I quit my day job and went to work for myself full time. Sure enough, I almost immediately had to hire help to keep up with the orders. Though I had only a few items for sale in my shop, people contacted us for all kinds of custom furniture. I found a niche that was in high demand and I found my customers, in many different online marketplaces. Within a couple of years, we had ten full-time employees and were making $50,000-$70,000 per month, with more than 80,000 website views per month and 2,000-4,000 views per day. Mt Hood Wood Works was off and running!

However, not everything went smoothly. It seemed that a problem lurked around every corner.

Little did I know that we would have so much to learn, and so many issues to overcome...

Introduction

This book is designed to be a straightforward guide to starting and growing your business. It includes information necessary to make your business successful. These are the exact methods we employed to make over $1.8 million, and to grow our shop sales to $70,000 per month.

As you have probably noticed, a multitude of information is available about how to sell online… but that's the problem. I've read many books about selling goods online and have found that, unfortunately, most are packed full of useless information. With all this information out there, how will you know what works? Only a handful of your methods will lead to REAL success. Some people might say that all it takes is hard work and sweat, but sometimes there's just "1 thing" that's preventing you from achieving your goal. This book is full of those "1 things." With this book, my goal is to give you a straight line to success, so that you don't have to waste your time with methods that don't provide results.

When I started in this business, it would have been so lovely if I could have found all the information I needed in one place. Over the years, we have figured out how to increase our sales when times are slow, and how to slow things down when they're moving too fast. We've learned how to create our listings so that they rank at the top of search results. We've learned how to get views and how to make sales. We searched for and found the answers we needed to keep going. When it comes to selling goods online, there are many "tricks of the trade."

List of things you will learn

-Your business plan: A critical recipe for success.

-SEO: Search Engine Optimization. 6 things you need to know.

-Listing images: 3 things you need to know.

-6 business policies that will put your shop on top.

-Branding: a necessary component.

-How to grow your business most effectively.

-How to reduce advertising costs and get the best ad rates available.

-How to ship your items inexpensively and get the best shipping rates.

-How to deal with customer issues, bad reviews, and returns.

-3 ways to minimize damage when you have problems with an order.

-3 ways to have bad reviews removed.

As well as these helpful checklists:

#1. Business start-up checklist.

#2. Income and expenses checklist.

#3. SEO management checklist.

#4. Advertising checklist.

#5. Final checklist.

Chapter 1
Recipe for Success

Do you have the ingredients?

Here is the recipe for your success. If you combine all these ingredients, you will have a prosperous online business. Your success depends on the following:

#1. The cost of your products, including overhead.
If you can keep your costs low, you will have a significant advantage!

#2. The amount of demand in the marketplace.
If your products are in demand, you're off to a great start!

#3. The amount of competition, and competitors' ability to compete with you.
I will give you the secrets to rise to the top!

#4. The ability to advertise and create optimal SEO conditions.

This book will show you how to get the most through SEO and advertising.

#5. Your business policies.
I will show you six policies that can put you on top!

#6. Customer satisfaction and reviews.
This one is entirely between you and your customers.

#7. Your attitude, ambition, and motivation to succeed.
Don't give up; you will succeed!

You can simply put a product up for sale on many websites and instantly you are in business. But wait! Let's walk through some common considerations for new business owners so that you start on the right foot.

To increase your odds of success, walk through the following checklist. Here's a basic list of things you may need to consider before you start your business:

Business Startup Checklist

- ☐ Supply. Do you have a product to sell? Do you need an inventory of products?
- ☐ Profit. What will your profit margin be?
- ☐ Workspace. Do you have a place/space where you can work?
- ☐ Adequate compensation. How much compensation do you want/need to make? (see income/expense worksheet)
- ☐ Tools/Equipment. Do you have all the tools, equipment, and supplies to get started?
- ☐ Startup expenses. Do you have any startup costs?

- ☐ Overhead. Do you have overhead? (e.g., building rent, utilities, insurance).
- ☐ Monthly expenses. Make a list of your monthly expenses and anticipated income (see income/expense worksheet).
- ☐ Business Type/Name. Which business type will you have (e.g., corporation, sole proprietorship, LLC)? Do you need to register your business?

It takes money to make money. Your profit margin will determine the percentage of profit you make after all your business expenses. Here's the formula. Sales minus expenses = profit. Profit divided by sales equals profit margin. (Your profit margin is the percentage of profit you receive from your items, after all costs, overhead, supplies, materials, etc.) For example: $5,000 in sales minus $4,000 in expenses equals $1,000 in profit. 1,000/5,000 = .20, which is a 20% profit margin.

You may want to mark up your merchandise by a certain percentage so that you can maintain a specific profit margin. Either way, it's good to know your profit margin on items. That way, you can see how much profit you're making. You may want to discontinue products with a low profit margin and advertise those products that have a higher profit margin.

#1. Calculate the profit margins on your products so you can see which are the most profitable.

#2. Maintain a healthy profit margin and look for ways to increase that margin.

#3. Stick with products that have high profit margins. Sometimes businesses can do well with low profit margins, but this can be dangerous. Your profit margin is like a cushion between success and failure.

If unexpected expenses arise, you may find your profit margin going into the negative.

Income and Expense Checklist

Write down your income (or anticipated income) and costs associated with each item in the list. Some of these expenses may not apply to your situation.

Income:
- ☐ expected gross sales
- ☐ other income

Expenses:
- ☐ building/space rent
- ☐ electricity
- ☐ gas
- ☐ garbage
- ☐ internet service
- ☐ tools/equipment
- ☐ business fixtures (desks, shelving, computers, etc.)
- ☐ computer software
- ☐ business insurance
- ☐ website startup fees
- ☐ business vehicle
- ☐ advertising fees
- ☐ travel costs
- ☐ materials/supplies
- ☐ shipping expenses
- ☐ payroll expenses
- ☐ products to sell/inventory
- ☐ quarterly tax payments

- ☐ business license
- ☐ business name registration
- ☐ other business setup fees
- ☐ lawyer fees
- ☐ personal expenses
- ☐ other business expenses

To see how much you will need to earn monthly, add up your current monthly expenses and your business expenses. Many businesses start small; they use their garage, or they use part of their house for a workspace, and they don't have a lot of expenses at first. Then, as they grow, they must expand their operations to accommodate a greater number of orders.

Be sure that you don't grow too fast! I've personally seen several businesses go under because they expanded too quickly. Not everyone has this problem. If you build your business slowly, you will be able to handle fluctuations in sales. You will also be more familiar with your typical monthly expenses, and you will be more prepared to handle your business's growth. If you take on more than you can manage, it could be a recipe for disaster.

Chapter 2

Getting Started

Getting an online presence up and running is easy. There are many websites where you can sell your products. List your products on the websites that are most applicable for your products. Here's a list of popular online marketplaces that may work for you:

-Amazon: #1 Best marketplace for selling a plethora of products. #1 for selling books.

-Etsy: #1 Best online marketplace for many handmade goods, crafts, vintage items, and art.

-eBay: Great marketplace for many different products.

-Craigslist: Another great site for many products. But beware of scammers.

-Bonanza: Similar to eBay, with many unique items.

-Create a website: Use Shopify, Wix, BigCommerce, or others to create an online store easily.

Research your niche, to find the best ways to sell your products. Using multiple online marketplaces for selling your items is recommended. This will help to increase your sales and improve your SEO ranking (more discussed later).

The process for setting up your online store is typically self-explanatory and user-friendly. Usually, the website will guide you through the entire process. But wait! Several steps will play a significant role in determining your success. Here they are:

Title, tags, and description/SEO optimization

SEO (Search Engine Optimization) isn't as complicated as you might think. Nor is it as complicated as people make it out to be. Many professionals would have you believe that only they know the secrets to get you to the top of the search results. However, chances are, they won't get you even close to the top. Here's what you need to know in 6 steps:

#1. Use the right keywords.

Using the right keywords and phrases in your listings is an essential component of SEO. Your listing title must describe your product and use the actual keywords for which your customers are searching. Use the "Google keyword research and strategy tool" to help with this task; it's currently at the following link:

http://adwords.google.com/home/tools/keyword-planner

With this tool, you can search for individual keywords associated with your products and see the amount of online traffic for each keyword. This tool is free; SEO professionals use it to write your tags, titles, descriptions, and everything else in your shop. Using these keywords will help your SEO tremendously!

#2. Use specific search terms.

Keywords with less traffic may get you more traffic. That's because generic and basic search terms have more competition. Use keywords and search terms that describe your product in detail. Then you will be more likely to get a sale when someone clicks on your listing. This will also do wonders for your placement in searches. Compile a list of appropriate and specific keywords and use them in your listing title, descriptions, and tags, as well as possibly in your shop name/shop about page. Don't forget your announcement; this is an essential aspect of your SEO. Your shop announcement should describe your shop, promote sales, and portray your shop's best qualities – and don't forget to include the keywords. Keyword repetition will take your products and shop higher in search results.

If your shop has many similar products, use different titles for each. For example, if you are selling tables, you could list one as a "restaurant table" and another as a "kitchen table." This way, you will reach different groups of people through each listing. However, be specific and descriptive. In your titles and search tags, use as many words as you can. Use descriptive words as well as words that let people know you have a premium product to sell.

#3. Get views that convert to sales.

The best way to optimize your page for searches is to convert your views to sales. (This is your conversion rate.) Search engines love to see a high conversion rate. The search engines will place you higher in their search results when they see that your views are relevant and ultimately result in sales. In your description, describe your product in detail; take your time and be thorough. The better you describe your product, the more sales you will get, and the fewer questions people will have.

#4. Update your shop regularly.

To achieve optimal SEO conditions for your website, you must consistently update/change your shop and products. Search engines regularly "crawl" websites; if you have made changes to your site, the search engines will know that your business is active and engaged, which will help put you toward the top of search results. To show the search engines that your page is active, you can add new keywords to your tags, create better descriptions, or add new products.

#5. Use all your tags/search terms.

Some websites will help you with your tags or automatically create them for you, based on your product information. Your search tags and keywords are a primary method through which people will find your products. For Search Engine Optimization, put your keywords in the following places:

#1. All sections of your shop,

#2. Your business name,

#3. Your product titles,

#4. Your product descriptions,

#5. Your "about" page and announcement.

Sometimes people will also be able to find your products through other search options (e.g., attributes, price, color, material type, shop location).

Use as many keywords, search terms, and descriptive words as possible! This is how your customers will find you. Otherwise, your shop will be lost in the abyss of online shops. That's why you must use your keywords everywhere possible. When you create your listing, fill it out as thoroughly as possible and choose as many options as you can so that customers will find your products.

#6. Use links and drive traffic to your shop through other sources.

If your shop is receiving traffic from multiple sources, the search engines will think you're famous and will like you more! Link your Facebook and Twitter page to your shop. Include links in your announcement and listing descriptions to show your customers where your product or shop is featured. Links to blogs, Reddit articles, and YouTube videos all work well. See the chapter on advertising to learn some of the best ways to drive traffic to your shop.

SEO Checklist

- Create a Google AdWords account and use the keyword planner tool to find your keywords.
- Create a list of specific keywords for your shop and products.
- Use these keywords in your business name, if possible.
- Use these keywords in your "about page," when applicable.
- Use these keywords in your shop announcement, when applicable.
- Use these keywords in your product titles.
- Use these keywords in your product descriptions.
- Use these keywords as your "tags" when you are creating your listings.
- Use as many keywords as possible.
- Be specific and descriptive.
- Use different titles for similar products.

- Try to make your views result in sales so that you can get a high conversion rate. This will tell the search engine that your listing was relevant to the person who clicked on it. This will also tell the search engine that the view of your listing was successful because it resulted in a sale.
- Update/change your shop regularly.
- Be thorough and fill out all options possible when creating your listings.
- Drive traffic to your shop through other sources (e.g., your Facebook page, advertising, blogs, Pinterest).
- Create a simple ad with Google AdWords. (This helps with Search Engine Optimization.)

Listing Images
"A picture is worth a thousand words."

Your product pictures are vital to making sales Some people won't even click on your listing if the main image isn't good. On the other hand, people will click on your listing simply because of the picture, even if they don't need the product. With that in mind, approach this step with a lot of consideration and care. Use as many images as you can. Sometimes people don't read a single word within your listing, but make a purchase based solely on what appears in your pictures.

#1. Use a high-quality camera, such as a "DSLR" - type camera. I know cell phones have decent cameras these days, but image quality is crucial.

#2. Use natural light. You can take your photos outside or next to a window, but make sure the lighting is perfect because Photoshop can do only so much. If you use Photoshop, make sure the product still looks the same, so that when the customer receives it, they are not confused about why it looks different than in your pictures.

#3. Use a "natural" or "typical" background. If you're selling art, hang it on the wall. If you're selling a doormat, put it in front of a door. Your customers want to know what the product will look like in the appropriate setting. Also, you can use a natural background. I frequently use a natural setting – with trees, rocks, foliage, and natural scenery – as a background, and it has worked well for us. We are required to use a solid white background for all products that we sell through Amazon and Houzz. A solid-color background works in some cases, but it's not my favorite. We have found success with all types of backgrounds; however, every product is different, so do what you think will work best for your products. Also, get feedback from others. Ultimately, the proof lies in the number of views and sales from your customers.

Policies

Create customer-friendly policies that will attract and satisfy buyers. Your policies can make you a leader in your field and increase the value of your products. Often, people will buy from you simply because you have a good return policy or because you have fast shipping. A good set of policies can put your shop at the top of your category. Look at other businesses in your industry and see what your competition is offering. This will give you ideas for standing out from the rest. Here are some great ways to put your shop at the top:

#1. "Free shipping." You can factor this into your price. Sometimes people will buy only products that have free shipping. Sometimes, "free shipping" can be used as a filter when people are searching for products.

#2. "Fast shipping." Nothing is better than receiving your order quickly. Sometimes people have tight schedules and need their orders fast.

#3. "Lifetime guarantee." People know they're getting a high-quality product when they have to purchase it only once in their entire life. This policy can add a significant amount of customer-perceived value.

#4. Money-back guarantee." Your customers will be more likely to buy if they know they can return the product if they don't want it.

#5. "All forms of payment accepted." Sometimes you can lose a customer simply because you don't accept PayPal or a personal check. Be careful of scams and cashier's checks. However, the more forms of payment you accept, the better.

#6. "Using recycled materials." We should be good caretakers of our environment. If your business uses recycled materials, you may find customers who appreciate this. Many people will pay a premium to support a good cause.

Here are some other considerations for your policies:

-Do you accept returns? Cancellations? Within how many days of purchase?

-What are the terms for refunds?

-What if the product is damaged in transit?

-Is shipping insurance included? Signature service?

-Do you offer local delivery? Or local pickup only?

Branding

If you want to stand out from other shops and gain recognition, you must create a "brand" for yourself. Your brand starts with your business name, your logo, a banner, and other unique attributes in your shop. Add something special to your pictures, like a symbol or phrase. Create a unique layout in your descriptions, or perhaps your policies are a novel component of your brand – one that sets you apart from the competition. Branding brings your customers back and familiarizes people with your business. It can be an essential aspect of success. Business cards, pamphlets, postcards, and other advertising materials can also be important components of your branding. It's a good practice to include a business card with every order. You could even include a special offer, such as 10% off for returning customers.

Chapter 3
Growing Your Shop

Now that your listings are in place, take some time to see what is working and which parts of your shop require a change. Always focus on the quality of your listings. You can sell more products with one great listing than you can with 100 mediocre ones. Also, the more products you have for sale, the more people will discover to buy. You can drive more traffic to your shop this way.

If you've received any sales, you're on the right track. The best way to grow your business is to increase your views. Increasing your views should always increase your sales. Like the saying goes: "There is no such thing as bad publicity." Here's a list of some of the most effective advertising methods.

Advertising Checklist

☐ Website Advertising *

Typically, the websites you use will offer their own advertising on their website and they will show your products when their customers are searching for related items. We keep our CPC (cost per click) at around .07-.15 cents per click. This advertising method usually costs us about 10% of our advertising sales (i.e., for $1,000 in sales, it costs us $100).

☐ Offer a Sale *

Here is an excellent method for increasing sales. It's free, and it usually doubles the number of transactions we get. We will lower our prices by 10% and put the following in our listing titles: "Limited Time Sale 10% off". We will typically run the sale from Friday through Monday afternoon.

☐ Google AdWords

- A Google ad will help with your placement on Google searches.

- You don't have to spend much to see SEO results.

- Overall, this is more expensive than the other types of advertising listed.

\- You can regularly find deals that offer $100 in free advertising when you open a new account.

☐ Facebook Page *

This is excellent free advertising, and it works very well. Highly recommended!

☐ Facebook Advertising *

Use this to build your following AND get sales. Due to consistent Facebook advertising, we currently have around 9,000 followers. We use a low CPC (cost per click), and we target a specific audience. You will have much success with this method if you can narrow down your audience to a group of people who are extremely likely to purchase from you. You can target an audience so that your ads are shown to people who live in a specific location, who have particular interests, are in specific age groups, and so much more. Highly recommended!

☐ Pinterest

Much free traffic has come to our site through Pinterest. This traffic is mostly from customers who have pinned our photos to their boards. Depending on the types of products you sell, you may have a large customer base that uses Pinterest.

- Reddit

Reddit articles regularly go viral and can generate massive views. If you create a presence on this site, you can drive a lot of traffic to your shop.

- Blogs

Contact people in your industry and ask if they can feature you on their blogs. You can also create your own blog and drive traffic for years.

We've seen much success through these channels, though some are easier to use than others. I've put a star next to those methods on which we have focused the most. The more work you put into these methods, the more views and sales you will get.

Our business has never been featured on a website, or in a popular news article, or even on a viral post. Our business growth has just stemmed from steady work and positive results.

Getting the most from your advertising

When we advertise through a "cost per click" method, we never go with the "automated bid." We start with the lowest price per click possible, then increase that number daily until we begin to see satisfactory results. Sometimes the automatic bid for cost per click advertising is over $1.00 per click, but I have found that we get surprising results at just $.07 per click!

All these listed advertising methods (free and paid) work incredibly well, but take time to perfect.

*I focus our advertising efforts between Friday afternoon and Monday afternoon. I would estimate that 80% of our sales have occurred during these times.

We grew our shop income to $70,000 per month and $1.8 million in total online sales. We have maintained a consistent number of sales since we opened. We could have kept growing, but instead we have found a steady pace of orders that is comfortable for us. We frequently have too many requests coming in and must raise our prices or temporarily extend our processing times. When we want more orders, we advertise, decrease our shipping/processing times, or run a "10% off" sale.

All these methods, if done correctly, can generate a substantial increase in sales.

I recommend having an AdWords account even if you spend only $1.00 per month or less. It is not my favorite advertising method, but this will help you get higher placement in the Google search results (which is great for SEO). I also recommend having your own website where people can find you. We have found success selling through eBay, Amazon, Craigslist, Etsy, Houzz, Shopify, and others. If you would like more business, expand your reach.

What do your customers want? Put yourself in their shoes. What search terms are they using to find you? How do they choose which products to buy? Don't advertise your products from a seller's point of view; to be successful, use your customers' point of view.

Keep in mind that this advertising list isn't a 100% complete list of ALL marketing channels or sales platforms. It is a list of popular platforms that have worked incredibly well for our business and for thousands of other online companies.

*Setting up all your accounts will take some time, but these efforts will pay off for years to come!

Chapter 4

Problems Arrive

Unhappy customers: Reviews and cases

Happy customers are necessary for success. Satisfied customers will leave good reviews and tell their friends and family to order from you. Before you know it, you will have people knocking down your doors. You will still have the occasional unhappy customer; there is no way around that. However, you can do certain things to minimize the damage.

#1. Purchase insurance for your shipments in case the shipping carrier loses your package. It happens. Respond to your customers' complaints right away.

#2. If your customer opens a chargeback against you, make sure you have followed your shop policies and the policies of the website that you sold the item through. Abiding by your shipping and processing times is important. And make sure you keep in contact with your customers if there will be any changes to their order. When a customer isn't happy with a product they've received, and they open a chargeback against you, you can usually win the case if you have fulfilled your obligations and treated your customer professionally.

#3. When your customer orders "custom-made" merchandise from you, you are not obligated to accept a return if you have indicated this in your policies. PayPal has similar policies; they will not require you to refund a custom order simply because the customer decides they don't want it. Sometimes a lot of work goes into a custom order, and if you deliver it as promised, you shouldn't have to refund the order.
    *Customer satisfaction is the most important thing; it should be the primary focus of every business.

More about reviews

When a customer leaves a bad review, sometimes you can have the marketplace remove it, and other times you can have the customer remove it. Here are a few instances where we've been successful.

#1. One time, we asked the marketplace to remove a negative review, and they did because the customer had left two identical reviews.

#2. Another time, we asked a customer to remove their review because we considered it defamatory. They had to call the marketplace, but they removed it for them.

#3. Also, if a customer is trying to get something of value in exchange for their review (extortion), you can have the marketplace remove it.

When a customer opens a chargeback, the marketplace will typically check to see if you have performed your obligations according to your shop policies and their policies. If you have, they will most likely rule in your favor, especially if you have treated your customer kindly and professionally.

There may come times when you must hold your ground. Always take control of situations and work to achieve your desired outcome. You have a right to stick up for what you believe in.

Also, the old saying, "The customer is always right," can go a long way when it comes to preventing additional problems. Remember, your customers have the right to leave an honest review, whether good or bad.

Copyright claims, DCMA

Copyright issues are serious; if other shops are copying anything from your shop, you may have recourse. Through a process known as the DCMA takedown notice, you can have any infringing material removed from the web almost immediately. Some marketplaces have their own method for this.

You may never have to put up with people copying your work again. The DCMA process is not complicated and takes no time at all. Make sure you follow necessary copyright regulations and contact a lawyer if you need help with patents, disclaimers, and registered trademarks, or even to look things over before you start your adventures. The following link contains **more information about the DCMA takedown notice and how it may apply to you:**

www.google.com/search?q=How+do+I+send+a+DMCA+takedown+notice

Chapter 5
Shipping

Pricing

A large percentage of our business consists of shipping. We have used USPS, FedEx, and UPS as our primary shipping carriers. Each company has its pluses and minuses. Here's where I've found the best deals.

-For small merchandise, USPS offers excellent pricing.

-For heavy merchandise, USPS offers great deals on flat rate boxes of specific sizes.

-For envelopes of all sizes, USPS usually has the best deals.

-For all other boxes and packages, UPS and FedEx will typically give you the best rates.

When you are getting started, make an appointment with a sales rep from UPS and FedEx. Inform them of the type and frequency of shipments you plan to make and get quotes for standard sizes. Make them compete for your business and show them the pricing that the other company is offering. See if one can beat the pricing of the other; go back and forth until you get the lowest pricing available. UPS and FedEx commonly compete against each other. They will most likely love to see the deal that their competitor is offering you. Typically, they will give you a counteroffer to win your business.

We pay a small weekly fee to have UPS and FedEx pick up our outgoing shipments every day. You can schedule a "daily pickup," or a pickup as needed. You can schedule pickups online or over the phone.

Packaging

Packaging materials can be re-used. You can usually find used boxes from local businesses to recycle. I've seen shops that use all kinds of household recyclable materials for fill and cushioning material; it's a lot better for the environment than Styrofoam. People appreciate "green" practices, and they may buy from you (instead of someone else) solely for that reason.

You can purchase custom-size boxes from many places. Home Depot and Lowes offer boxes at excellent prices, but only in certain sizes. If you want the ability to file a claim, your shipping carrier may require a particular type of box, so ask your sales rep about their requirements.

Customer considerations

Shipping your orders on time is extremely important. Most of our negative reviews relate to our not meeting shipping/processing times.

Insuring your shipments can save you when your item is damaged or lost in transit. Opening a claim to receive reimbursement for a lost package is not an easy process; yet while it's time-consuming, it will prevent you and your customer from losing money. I recommend getting insurance on all your shipments so you will receive reimbursement to replace the item if the carrier damages or loses it.

Equipment and software

Your shipping sales rep should give you a shipping label printer for a small fee. They will also give you rolls of free shipping labels. In addition, they should help you set up the printer software on your computer.

We use shipping software called "Shipstation." Shipstation charges a monthly fee to automatically upload all your orders to its website, where you can easily print labels for any order at the click of a button. This software saves much time when it comes to printing labels. Inputting information manually to print a label takes a lot of time. Shipstation can save you hours every day.

Final Checklist

- Did you set up your business entity?
- Do you have business insurance coverage?
- Are your products reasonably priced?
- How does your shop rank against your competition?
- Do you have several products listed?
- Do your item descriptions include answers to common questions?
- Do your titles, descriptions, and tags have the right keywords/phrases?
- Do your titles, descriptions, and tags describe your products clearly?
- Does your shop announcement have keywords/promote sales?
- Do you have an attractive shop logo which relates to your industry?
- Are your policies thorough and do you have remedies for issues?
- Is your "about" page complete, as well as warm and friendly?
- Did you set up your Facebook and Twitter pages?
- Do your listings have plenty of quality pictures?
- Have you posted photos of your products on Pinterest?
- Did you set up a Google AdWords account?

- Have you researched keywords using the Google keyword planner?
- Have you set up a small Google ad for advertising?
- Are your ads dialed in at a minimum CPC?
- Have you tried a sale?
- Have you negotiated shipping rates and scheduled daily pickup, if needed?
- Are you selling your products through multiple online marketplaces?
- Is your workspace set up to maximize efficiency? Is it safe?

Chapter 6

Final Words

Remember, attitude is everything. Treat your customers well and they will thank you for your service. Be positive when problems arise and focus on finding a solution. Work hard and you will be successful. Never give up and you will not fail.

Always try to have a good time. Treat yourself well. Treat your employees and contractors well. Make the experience pleasurable for everyone involved. If you don't enjoy your work, maybe you're in the wrong business.

When you are determining your pricing, remember that people will pay more for an item if they know it will arrive in one piece and if they feel comfortable with your process. Sometimes your customers will choose you over your competitors simply because your pictures or reviews are better. You don't have to be the cheapest to be the most successful.

Continue to learn. The more knowledge you have about your industry, the greater the advantage you will have over your competition.

"Our greatest weakness lies in giving up. The most certain way to succeed is always to try just one more time." —Thomas Edison

"It does not matter how slowly you go as long as you do not stop." —Confucius

"Never give up on a dream just because of the time it will take to accomplish it. The time will pass anyway." —Earl Nightingale

Thank you for choosing this short book. If you liked it, please leave a review on Amazon. I hope you will be able to easily apply the methods discussed and may it lead you down the road of long-term success.

Mike Raft

Online business owner

mikeraftauthor@gmail.com

www.ingramcontent.com/pod-product-compliance
Lightning Source LLC
Chambersburg PA
CBHW030956240526
45463CB00017B/2740